It's Easy To Play Strauss.

Wise Publications
London/New York/Sydney

Exclusive Distributors:
Music Sales Limited
8/9 Frith Street, London W1V 5TZ, England.
Music Sales Corporation
257 Park Avenue South, New York, NY 10010, USA.
Music Sales Pty Limited
120 Rothschild Avenue, Rosebery, NSW 2018, Australia.

This book © Copyright 1991 by Wise Publications
Order No. AM83791
ISBN 0.7119.2553.4

Cover art direction by Michael Bell Design.
Cover illustration by Paul Leith.
Compiled by Peter Evans.
Arranged by Barry Todd.
Music processed by Bill Pitt Music Services.
Typeset by Capital Setters.

Music Sales' complete catalogue lists thousands of titles and
is free from your local music shop, or direct from Music Sales Limited.
Please send a cheque/postal order for £1.50 for postage to:
Music Sales Limited, Newmarket Road, Bury St. Edmunds, Suffolk IP33 3YB.

Your Guarantee of Quality
As publishers, we strive to produce every book to
the highest commercial standards.

All the music has been freshly engraved, and the book has
been carefully designed to minimise awkward page turns and
to make playing from it a real pleasure.

Particular care has been given to specifying acid-free, neutral-sized paper which
has not been elemental chlorine bleached but produced with special regard for the environment.
Throughout, the printing and binding have been planned to
ensure a sturdy, attractive publication which should give years of enjoyment.

If your copy fails to meet our high standards, please inform us
and we will gladly replace it.

Printed in the United Kingdom by
Caligraving Limited, Thetford, Norfolk.

Annen Polka

Op.117

Composed by Johann Strauss II

D.C. al ⊕ Coda

Coda ⊕

'Die Fledermaus'

Overture to the Operetta, Op.362

Composed by Johann Strauss II

Tales From The Vienna Woods

Waltz, Op.325

Composed by Johann Strauss II

Emperor Waltz

Op.437

Composed by Johann Strauss II

18

Pizzicato Polka

Composed by Johann Strauss II and Josef Strauss

Roses From The South

Waltz, Op.388

Composed by Johann Strauss II

Introduction

Waltz 2.

Thunder And Lightning Polka

Op.324

Composed by Johann Strauss II

The Blue Danube

Waltz, Op.314

Composed by Johann Strauss II

Tritsch Tratsch Polka

Op.214

Composed by Johann Strauss II

Tempo di Polka

Vienna Blood

Waltz, Op.354

Composed by Johann Strauss II

Wine, Women And Song

Waltz, Op.333

Composed by Johann Strauss II

12/02 (46151)